Computer Training
Windows 10

Kevin Wilson

www.elluminetpress.com

Computer Training: Windows 10

Publisher: Elluminet Press
Director: Kevin Wilson
Lead Editor: Steven Ashmore
Technical Reviewer: Mike Taylor, Robert Ashcroft
Copy Editors: Joanne Taylor, James Marsh
Proof Reader: Robert Price
Indexer: James Marsh
Cover Designer: Kevin Wilson

eBook versions and licenses are also available for most titles. Any source code or other supplementary materials referenced by the author in this text is available to readers at

www.elluminetpress.com/resources

For detailed information about how to locate your book's source code, go to

www.elluminetpress.com/resources

Table of Contents

About the Author

Kevin Wilson, a practicing computer engineer and tutor, has had a passion for gadgets, cameras, computers and technology for many years.

After graduating with masters in computer science, software engineering & multimedia systems, he has worked in the computer industry supporting and working with many different types of computer systems, worked in education running specialist lessons on film making and visual effects for young people. He has also worked as an IT Tutor, has taught in colleges in South Africa and as a tutor for adult education in England.

His books were written in the hope that it will help people to use their computer with greater understanding, productivity and efficiency. To help students and people in countries like South Africa who have never used a computer before. It is his hope that they will get the same benefits from computer technology as we do.

Acknowledgements

Thanks to all the staff at Luminescent Media & Elluminet Press for their passion, dedication and hard work in the preparation and production of this book.

To all my friends and family for their continued support and encouragement in all my writing projects.

To all my colleagues, students and testers who took the time to test procedures and offer feedback on the book

Finally thanks to you the reader for choosing this book. I hope it helps you to use your computer with greater ease.

Chapter 1

What's New in Windows 10

Windows 10 fixes a lot of the irritations found in Windows 8 by improving the interface for desktop computers and laptops, including the return of the Start menu, a virtual desktop system, and the ability to run Windows Store apps within a window on the desktop rather than in full-screen mode.

Windows 10 is a universal platform that runs across all devices such as Windows Phones, surface tablets, servers, data centres and games consoles.

The minimum PC hardware specification you would need is

1 GHz or faster processor (CPU)

2 GB Memory (RAM)

20 GB Hard Disk Space

Windows 10 Editions

Microsoft has released Windows 10 in a number of different editions aimed at the types of users and devices.

Windows 10 Home

This is the version that will ship with most home PCs, Laptops and larger tablets.

Windows 10 Pro

This is the successor to Windows 7 Professional and Windows 8 Professional editions and is aimed at business users, and allows users to connect to business networks, domains and access shared resources on a network.

Windows 10 Mobile

This edition is designed for phones and small tablets less than about 8" and will include most of the core features

Windows 10 Mobile Enterprise Edition

This is similar to the mobile edition mentioned above except it is aimed at businesses and is volume licensed.

Windows 10 Enterprise

This is essentially Windows 10 Professional as described above except aimed at large companies and businesses with a large number of users/workstations and comes with volume licensing.

Windows 10 Education

This is a new edition that focuses on educational establishments such as schools, colleges and universities and is available through academic volume license making it easier for schools to access.

Windows 10 IoT Core

This is a new edition of Windows 10 that will run on micro devices such as the Raspberry Pi

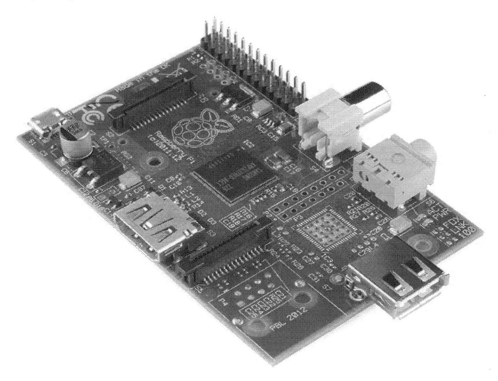

New Features

Here are some of the new features introduced in Windows 10

Start Menu

The familiar Start menu is back, but it brings with it a new customizable space for your favourite apps and Live Tiles.

Your most frequently used apps are listed down the left hand side as well as any recently added.

At the bottom you can click 'all apps' to reveal an alphabetical list of apps installed in your system

On the right hand side you have a selection of tiles that represent apps

The start menu can run as a menu in the bottom left hand side of the screen for desktop point and click environments or it can run as full screen which is better optimised for touch screen devices such as tablets.

Everything Runs in a Window

Apps from the Windows Store now open in the same format that desktop apps do and can be resized and moved around, and have title bars at the top allowing for maximize, minimize, and close with a click.

Snap Enhancements

You can now have four apps snapped on the same screen with a new quadrant layout.

Windows will also show other apps and programs running for additional snapping and even make smart suggestions on filling available screen space with other open apps.

New Task View Button

There's a new task-view button on the taskbar for quick switching between open files and quick access to any desktops you create.

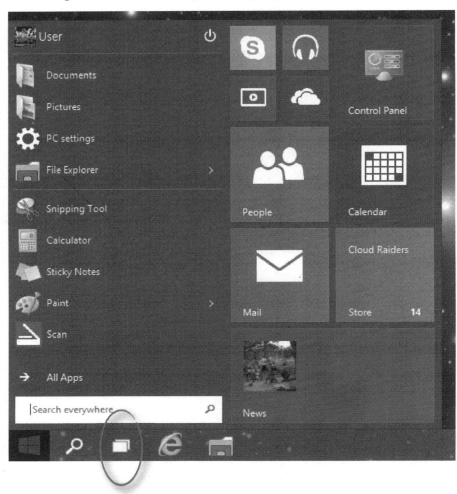

Multiple Desktops

Create desktops for different purposes and projects and switch between these desktops easily and pick up where you left off on each desktop.

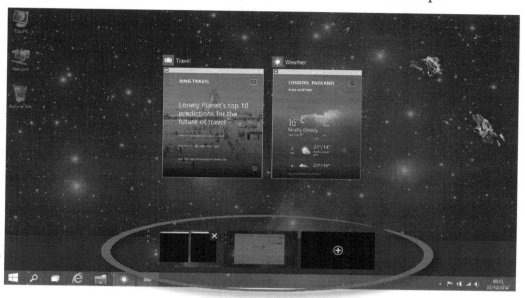

Find Files Faster

File Explorer now displays your recent files and frequently visited folders making for finding files you've worked on is easier.

One Windows: Multiple Devices

As mentioned earlier, Windows 10 is a universal platform that runs across all your devices:

Some common devices Windows 10 runs on

- Windows Phones

- Tablets

- Desktop PCs

- Laptops, Netbooks and Notebooks

- Servers

- Data centres

- Games consoles such as XBox

And even credit card sized computers such as the Raspberry Pi, MinnowBoard Max or Intel's Galileo.

Continuum

For convertible devices, such as the Surface, there are two modes, tablet and desktop.

When using the device as a tablet, Windows 10 will automatically change to tablet mode which is more touch-friendly.

This means apps will run full screen and allow you to use touch gestures to navigate.

Once you connect a mouse and keyboard, or flip your laptop around, Windows will go into desktop mode.

Apps turn back into desktop windows that are easier to move around with a mouse and you'll see your desktop again.

Introducing Cortana

Cortana is a voice activated digital assistant and comes with Windows 10.

There's a Cortana box on the taskbar where you can type, or tap the Cortana circle to see a welcome pane with your news, interests, weather.

You can tap the microphone icon to talk to Cortana

Introducing Microsoft Edge Web Browser

Codenamed "Spartan", Microsoft Edge is Microsoft's new web browser replacing Internet Explorer.

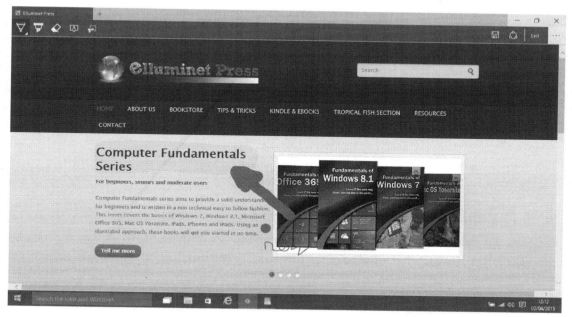

A lot more light weight than its predecessor and allows you to annotate and share these with others on the web.

New Calendar App

A new calendar app that allows you to link into your outlook calendar and your email address and now runs in a window rather than full screen.

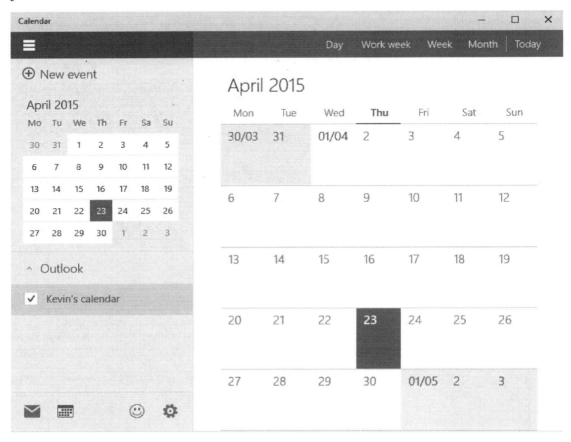

New Mail App

The new mail app has had a facelift and allows you to link in with your outlook email or your microsoft account email address.

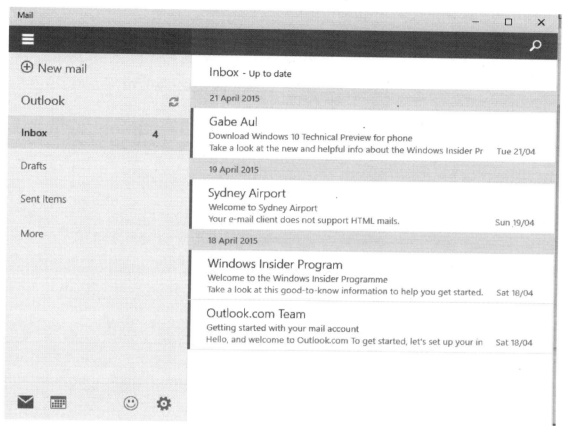

The Hololens

Microsoft HoloLens is a fancy headset that gives you the power to drop virtual screens onto walls, visit distant locations in person and add apps to anywhere in your home.

Turn your house, office and anywhere else you find yourself into a fully interactive digital hub for work, play and creativity.

Windows HoloLens is a new standalone device and doesn't need a PC to run

Setting up
Windows 10

Most new devices and computers will come with Windows 10 already installed but if you are running and older system such as Windows 7 or Windows 8 you will need to upgrade your system to Windows 10.

Microsoft have tried to make this as easy as possible by offering an app called 'Get Windows 10' that allows you to download the update from the App Store.

Windows 8, Windows 7 Home and Premium users will get Windows 10 Home.

Windows 8 and Windows 7 Professional will get Windows 10 Professional

In this section we'll try and guide you through setting up Windows 10.

Plus we'll cover a few tips and tricks to make using Windows 10 a little easier.

Upgrading to Windows 10

Windows 10 will be available free of charge to current Windows 7 & 8 users for the first year of release.

Desktop Computers & Tablets

If you have your automatic updates on, windows will prompt you to reserve a copy of windows 10 or download your copy.

You should be able to find the invitation by going to Windows Update.

You will receive an icon on the bottom right of your screen that looks like the windows logo. This is the Get Windows 10 app (GWX).

If you click this icon you'll get some instructions on what to do

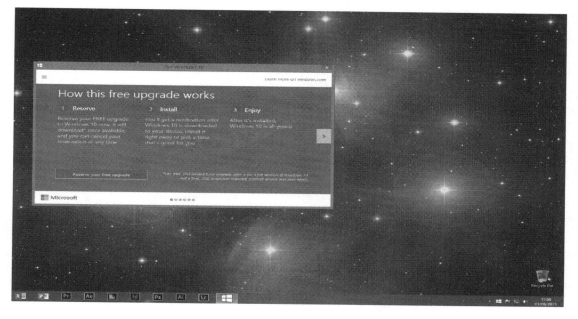

One you click download and install, Windows 10 will automatically upgrade your computer.

Running Windows 10 the First Time

Regional Settings

Select your country, language, keyboard layout for your country and your time zone.

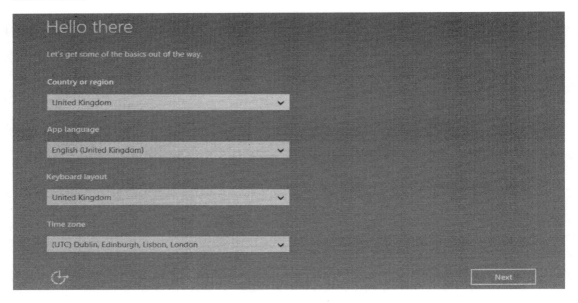

Terms Of Use

On the terms and agreements page click on accept

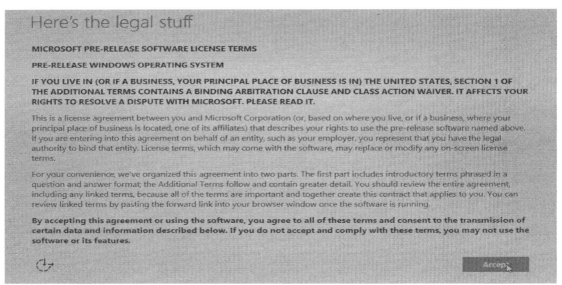

Connect to your WiFi

Select your WiFi network from the list of detected networks. This is usually printed on your router/modem or you can find out from your service provider.

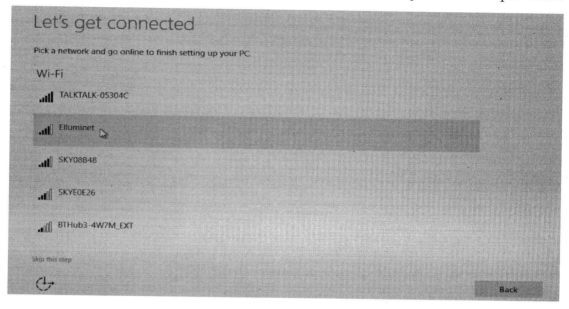

Enter WiFi Password

Enter the password for your WiFi network. This will be printed on the back of your router/modem or you can find out from your service provider.

Customise Settings

Click 'use express settings'. This will set your preferences to the most common, eg security settings, search engine preferences, location, etc

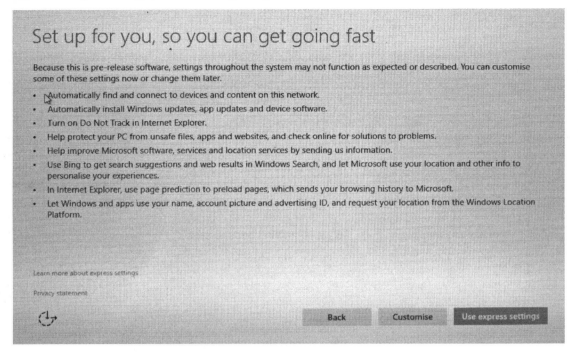

If you want to change any of these settings, eg use google instead of bing you can click customise then follow the step by step guide and select the appropriate option for each setting.

Select Network Options

If you are at home on a private network then click 'yes'. This will allow Windows 10 to scan your home network for other devices such as printers, other computers, laptops, phones or tablets you might also have.

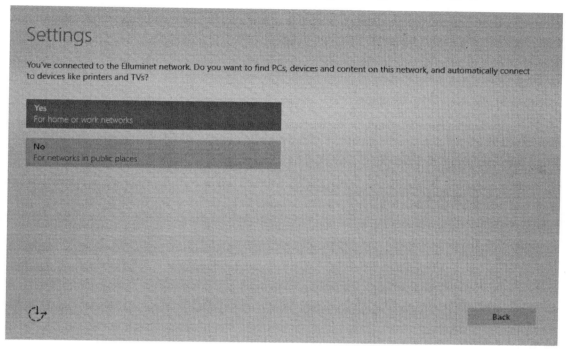

If you are connecting to a shared hotspot or public network in a library, school, coffee shop etc then select 'no'. This will help keep your computer more secure from anyone else that might be on the same network.

Select the Type of Network

If you are using your computer at home then select 'This device belongs to me'. This will allow you to connect to your home network or wifi

If you are using your computer at work and at home, select 'This device belongs to my company'. This allows you to sign in using the username and password given to you at work, school or college.

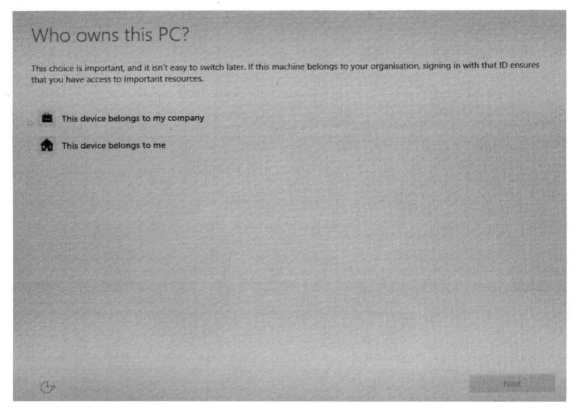

The difference is if you tell Windows 10 your device belongs to your company, you can access your company IT services, information, data and security policies.

Sign in for the First Time

To use Windows 10 Microsoft recommend you use a Microsoft Account, this allows you to make use of OneDrive, Email, purchase Apps from the App store, buy music and films.

If you have a Microsoft Account email and password enter them here on the left hand side of the screen.

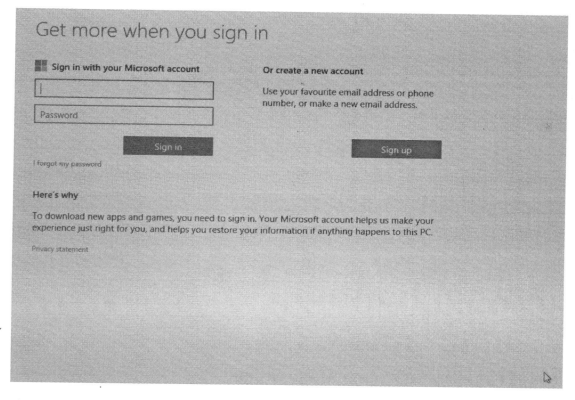

If you don't have one, you can click sign up and create one.

Create a Microsoft Account

Here, enter your first and second names then type in a username. This username will become your email address you use to sign into your Microsoft Account.

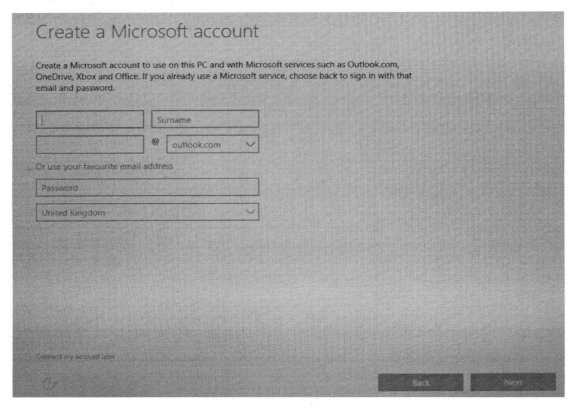

Enter a password and your country of residence.

Click next to create a computer account.

Enter your first name and choose a password.

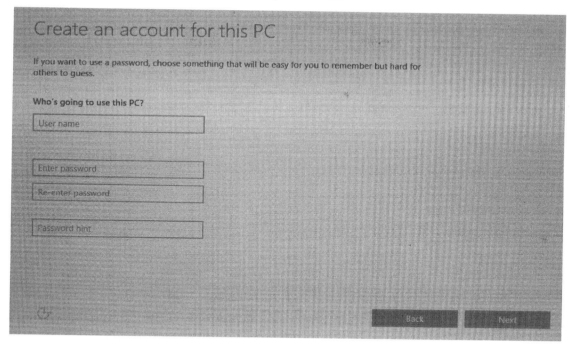

Click next

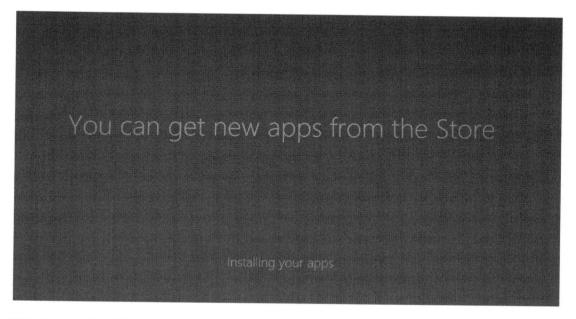

Windows 10 will now configure your account. This will take a few minutes.

Once you see the desktop you may need to switch to your Microsoft Account if Windows doesn't do it for you.

To do this go to the start menu and select settings on the top left.

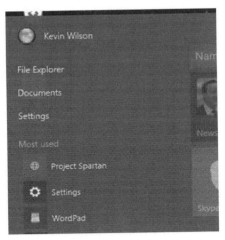

From the settings dialog box that appears select accounts. If you see 'Local Account' then click 'Sign in with a Microsoft Account'.

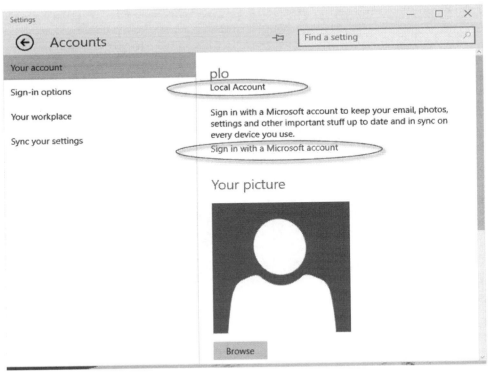

Follow the on screen instructions. Enter your Microsoft Account email address and password when prompted.

Customising Windows 10 Desktop

It is a good idea to customise Windows 10 to your personal preferences and needs.

Add Tiles to Start Menu

You can add tiles by dragging the icon off the list of apps on the left hand side of the start menu as shown below.

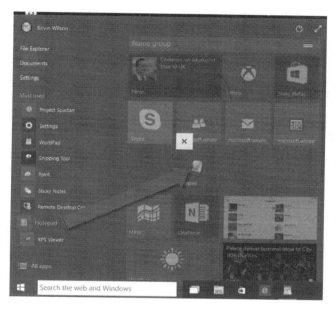

A good tip is to only drag your most used apps to tiles on your start menu. In this way you can build up a start menu where you can easily access all the apps you use the most without having to scroll through apps on your start menu. This is particularly useful if you happen to have a lot of apps installed on your machine.

If the app you want to add to your start menu is not listed, you can search for it using the search field on your start menu.

In this example I want to add the app called 'wordpad' to the start menu. I can search for it using the search field. When windows finds the app it will list it under a heading called 'Apps'.

Right click on the app icon and from the menu that appears select 'pin to start'

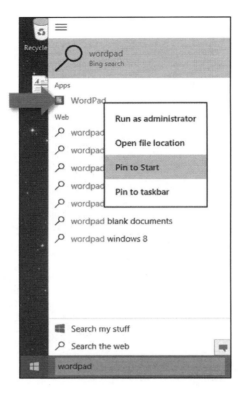

Move Tiles on the Start Menu

You can move tiles by clicking and dragging them to a new position. The tiles will scroll automatically as you drag your tile up and down the menu.

If you are on a touch screen device tap and hold your finger on the tile for a second then drag your finger up the screen to the position you want your tile.

Remove Tiles from Start Menu

You can remove tiles you don't use by right clicking on the tile and selecting 'unpin from start'

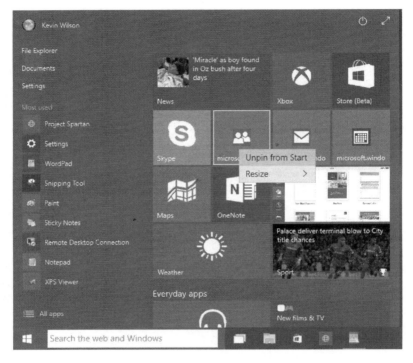

If you are on a touch screen device, tap and hold your finger on the tile until the menu appears.

Resize Tiles on Start Menu

You can resize tiles on the start menu by right clicking on the tile and selecting resize. You will see that each tile as a number of pre-set sizes (small, medium, wide & large).

Select the size from the drop down menu.

If you are on a touch screen device, tap and hold your finger on the icon and select resize.

User Settings

User settings can be found by clicking 'settings' on the top left of the start menu.

Here's a summary of the different options you have.

System	Display settings, screen resolution
Devices	Add printers, USB devices such as mouse/touchpad, enable autoplay features eg open dvd player automatically when dvd disc inserted.
Network & Internet	Connect to WiFi, or Ethernet/Cable internet, change internet options or enable flight mode which disables all wireless communications.
Personalisation	Change lock screen wallpaper/photo, set screensavers, desktop wallpaper, system sounds
Accounts	Manage user accounts, change passwords, create additional users, change profile photos etc
Time & Language	Set local time and regional settings such as date/time format, time zones, US or UK keyboard or language settings, foreign languages
Ease of Access	Useful for partially sighted or hard of hearing users. Allows you to magnify text or narrate screens and settings etc.
Privacy	Control access to devices, eg webcam, mic, smartscreen filter to help with internet security, enable or disable access to your physical location
Update & Recovery	Windows update, file backups, refresh or re-install windows, etc

Setting up Users

You can set up multiple users on your computers for different people on your computer.

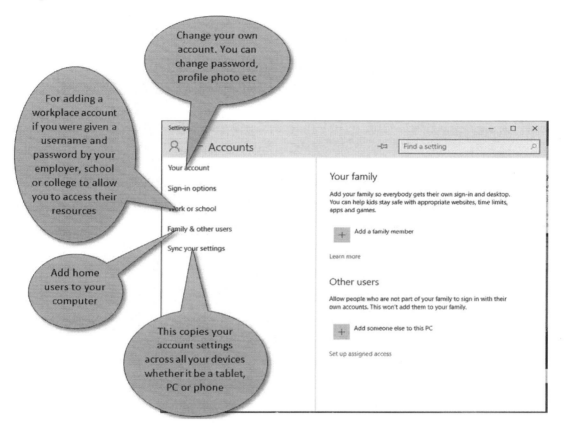

Users can have different privileges:

Administrators can install software and change settings.

Standard users are best for everyday computing needs.

Child users are monitored and reported to and 'adult' user.

Adding a New User

On the start menu select settings

From the settings dialog box select accounts.

Select 'family & other users'

Click 'add someone else to this PC'

Enter the user's Microsoft account email address and password.

If they don't have one, click 'sign up for a new email address' and enter their details.

Child Accounts

From the 'family & other users' accounts menu select 'add a family member'

Select 'add a child' and enter their email address

Click confirm

Children's accounts give parents the ability to block certain services or monitor their child's online activity.

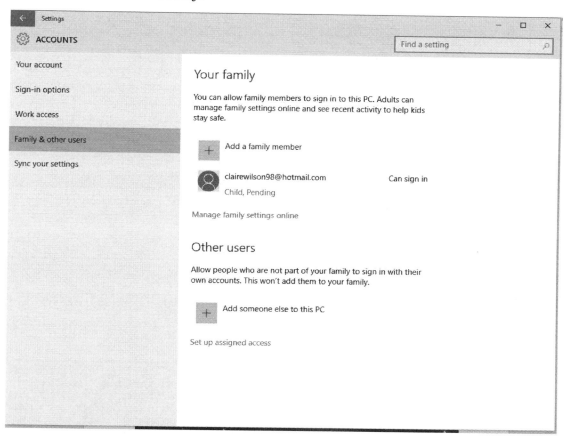

Sign in to their computer or tablet with the Microsoft Account username and password you just created.

A confirmation email will be sent the child's email address inviting them to sign in.

Check their email.

Kevin has invited you to join their Microsoft Family as a child.

 Microsoft Family (microsoftfamily@microsoft.com) 🟣 12:58 ▷ Newsletters
To: CLAIREWILSON98@HOTMAIL.COM ⌄

 Microsoft

Kevin has invited you to join their Microsoft Family as a child.

Sign in and accept

If you accept, the adults in your family can help make sure you stay safe online while giving you the freedom to explore and do things on your own. Otherwise, this invitation will expire in 14 days.

To learn more, visit

Microsoft respects your privacy. To learn more, read our

Microsoft Online Services
One Microsoft Way
Redmond, WA, 98052 USA

In the email click 'sign in and accept'

In the explorer window that appears

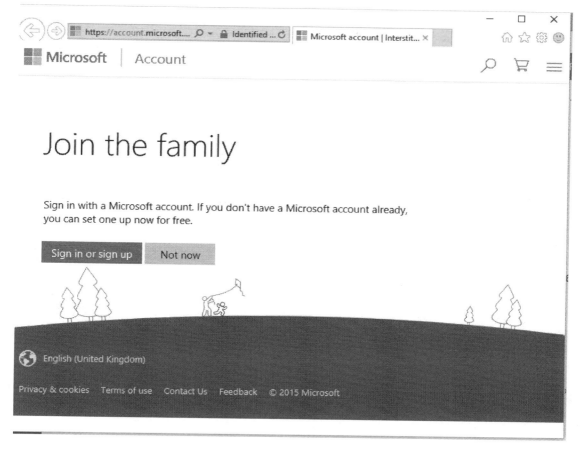

Click sign in

Family Safety

You can log on to your family safety website by opening your web browser and navigating to the following address.

```
http://account.microsoft.com/family
```

You can click on your child's name to view their activity.

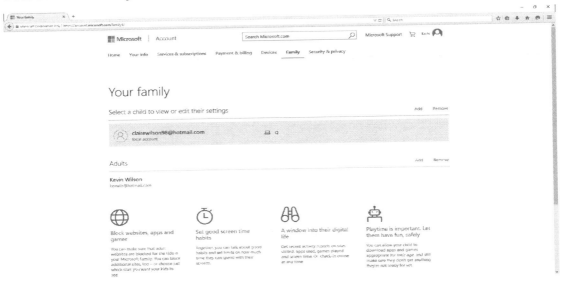

Websites visited are listed along with apps used and the number of hours they have been using the computer or tablet.

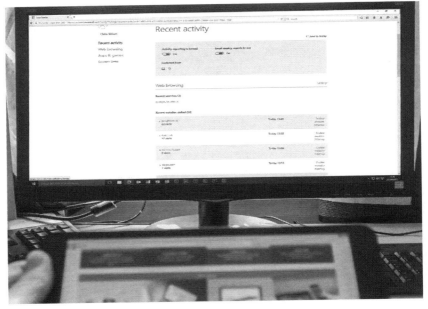

You can see in the background of the photograph the activity shown on my PC's monitor for Claire's tablet.

You can block websites by clicking on the 'web browsing' link down the left hand side of the screen

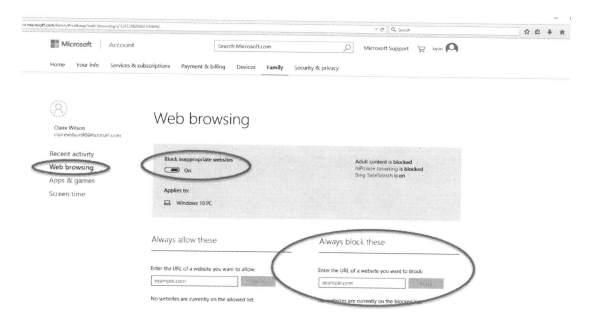

Turn on 'block inappropriate websites'. You can also add specific website addresses in the field 'always block these'

You can do the same with Apps & Games. Clicking on this link will allow you to set age limits on games. Eg, only allow your children to play 12s or block 18+ or adult games containing violence or sexual content.

Screen time allows you to set curfews so you can prevent your children using their tablets or computers except in the designated hours. Eg from 6pm-8pm. Or for 2 hours a day.

Set Up a Microsoft Account using Web

You can sign up online by launching your web browser and going to the following address

```
http://signup.live.com
```

Fill in the form scroll down and click accept at the bottom.

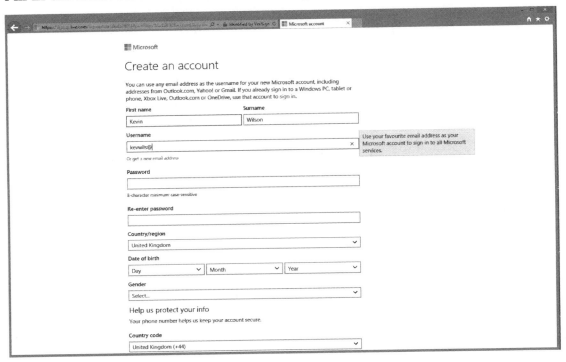

Set up OneDrive

OneDrive comes with Windows 10 and is probably the safest place to store all your files as they are backed up in case your PC crashes.

If you signed into Windows 10 with your Microsoft Account, then OneDrive is usually set up.

You can check by left clicking on OneDrive's icon in the system tray on the bottom right hand side of the screen.

Click get started.

Sign in with your Microsoft Account if prompted.

OneDrive will ask you where you want to store your OneDrive files on your computer while you work on them. Most of the time you can just leave it in it's default location. Click next.

OneDrive will scan for directories and files on your OneDrive account and ask you to copy them onto your local machine.

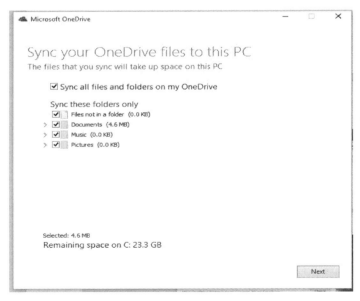

I usually select all of them. Click next.

The theory is, you work on the files on your local machine, edit, update, create save and do the things you need to do. Then OneDrive will copy these updates into your OneDrive Account on the Cloud so you can access them from any of your devices such as tablet, phone or on the web. This is called synchronisation.

You can find all your files on OneDrive by launching your File Explorer and scrolling down to the OneDrive section on the left hand side of the screen.

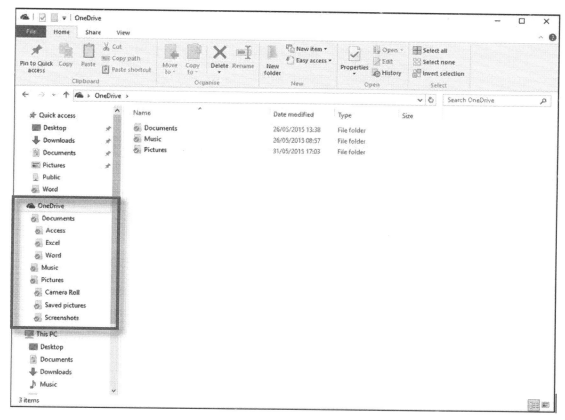

Windows 10 Tablets

This is what you'll see if you are running Windows 10 on a tablet in tablet mode.

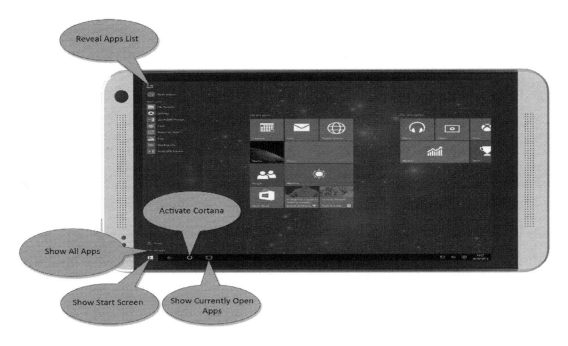

Along the left hand side you have a list of apps. Tap the hamburger icon on the very top left of the screen to reveal the list.

On the right hand side of the start screen you will see an array or coloured tiles. These represent your apps. You can tap these to start them up.

Along the bottom of the start screen, you'll see a black bar. From here you can tap the start screen icon, start Cortana personal assistant, tap the task view icon to show currently open apps.

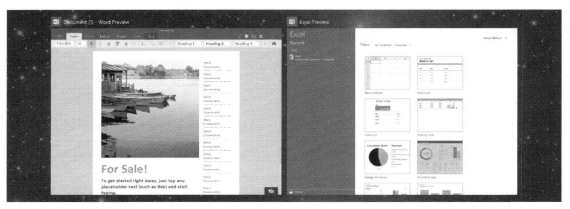

Customising your Start Screen

You can customise your start screen by resizing or moving tiles around. Just tap and slide your finger across the screen to where you want to place the tile.

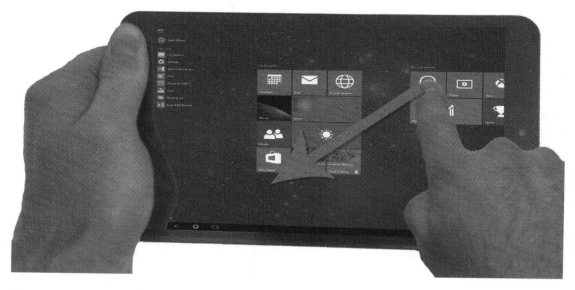

You can also drag your most used apps from the app list from the left hand side of the screen.

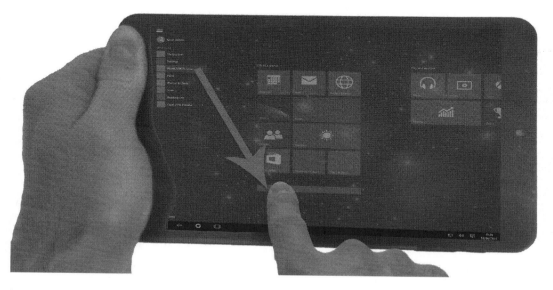

Tap 'all apps' on the bottom left if you don't see them all.

You can also resize tiles by tapping on the tile with two fingers

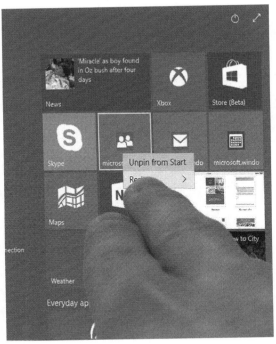

From the pop up menu tap resize. Then tap the size you want: small, medium, wide or large.

Using Windows 10

With Windows 10, Microsoft has tried to repair the damage caused by Windows 8. Windows 8 wasn't very well received and it alienated a lot of users in its attempt to unify touch screen devices and traditional point and click desktop environments.

The most notable change is the return of the Start Menu on the desktop/laptop point and click versions of Windows 10.

In this chapter we will take a look at the new features, how to get the most out of them and how to use the common features of Windows 10 to get your work done.

Start Menu

The start menu returns in Windows 10 with a few enhancements.

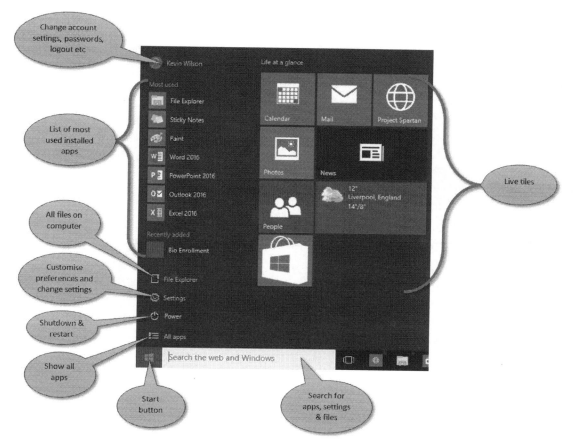

Listed down the left hand side of your menu, you'll see a list of your most frequently used applications. At the bottom of your list there is an option to show all the apps. This will list them down the left hand side of the start menu in alphabetical order.

On the right hand side of the menu, you'll see coloured tiles representing apps. If you have used Windows 8 you will be familiar with these.

A good tip is to drag your most used applications from the list on the left hand side of the start menu. This allows for quickness and eases your work flow.

The start menu can be displayed as a menu on the bottom left hand side of your screen and is better suited to point and click desktop users. Or your start menu can fill the whole screen putting more emphasis on the application tiles on the right hand side. This is useful for touch screen users using tablets and phones.

Task Bar

The task bar has two new options, one is the cortana/windows search box. This allows you to search for anything on your device or ask cortana a question.

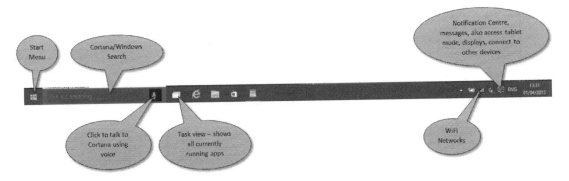

The other button is the task view option that allows you to see currently running apps, enables you to switch to that app by tapping on its icon or create a new virtual desktop.

The other notable addition is the notification centre.

File Explorer

File explorer can be used to find your files on your computer, access your OneDrive, network resources and external hard drives or flash drives.

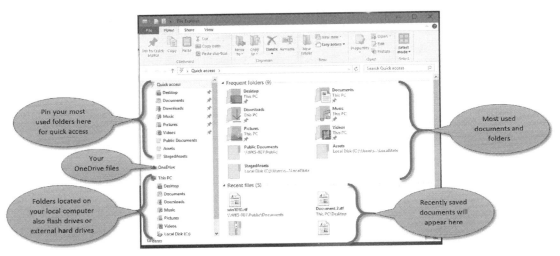

Different Devices Using Continuum

Windows 10 is designed to run seamlessly on all your devices, whether you are using a phone, tablet, xbox, laptop/notebook or desktop PC, Windows 10 will automatically select the correct mode for your phone or tablet with a touch screen interface or a desktop/laptop PC with a point and click interface.

Desktop PC/Laptop

Windows 10 is capable of running on a full sized desktop computer or workstation and runs in a similar way to Windows 7 did back in its day, with the start menu available to access your files and programs.

Tablets

You can easily switch to tablet mode where apps show up full screen and are a bit larger for a touch screen device.

You can see that in tablet mode everything opens up in full screen. The start menu becomes a start screen allowing you to use a touch interface.

In desktop mode, you see the start menu and everything runs in a window which is easier with a point and click keyboard and mouse interface.

If you own a tablet similar to the one pictured here you can buy cases that include a keyboard.

This allows you to use the device as a tablet but can also double as a touch screen notebook.

You can buy little USB adapters that plug into the side of your tablet. This allows you to plug in standard USB devices such as a mouse, digital camera, card reader, printer, etc.

This can be quite useful for those on the move all the time.

Phone

Windows 10 on a phone consists of a number of coloured tiles that represent the apps you have installed.

You can access Cortana, run Microsoft Edge web browser and a touch screen version of Microsoft Office for Windows 10.

You wont see that desktop or start menu on this version but you'll be able to access all your apps from the Start Screen as shown above.

Gestures for Touch Screens

One Finger Tap

Tapping with one finger is equivalent to clicking with your mouse, usually to select something. Tapping twice with your finger is the same as double clicking with the mouse and is usually used to start an app.

Two Finger Tap

Tapping on the screen with two fingers is equivalent to using the right click with the mouse and usually invokes a context menu

Three Finger Tap

Tapping on the screen with three fingers at the same time will invoke Cortana personal assistant.

Four Finger Tap

Tapping on the screen with four fingers at a time will invoke your command centre with your options, messages and notifications.

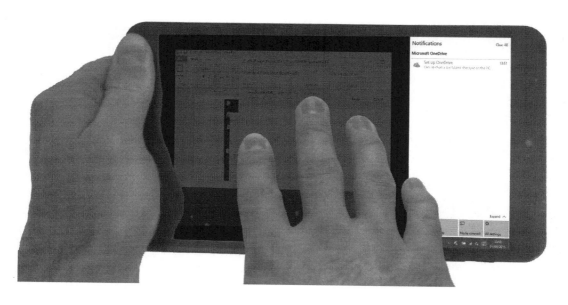

One Finger Tap + Slide

If you tap on the screen and slide your finger over the glass. This is the same as click and drag and you can use this to move your pointer or move objects on the screen.

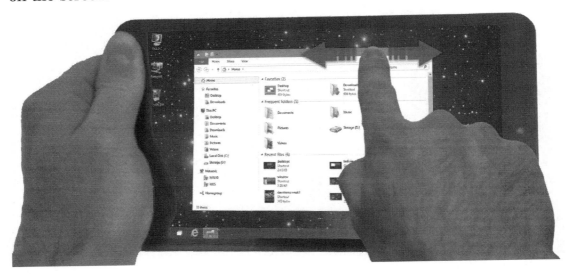

Two Finger Pinch

Pinch when used with your forefinger and thumb you can use to zoom into documents or maps and enlarge pages by zooming into and out of the screen.

Two Finger Scroll

If you tap and move two fingers over the glass as shown below you can scroll down documents and pages.

Three Finger Swipe

Swiping three fingers left and right across the screen will flick through open applications running on your device.

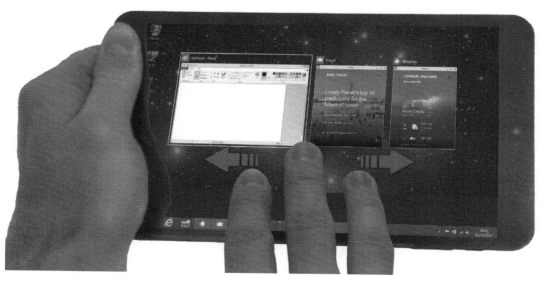

Using Cortana

Cortana is Microsoft's voice activated, personal assistant . You can use Cortana to set reminders using your natural voice rather than predefined commands.

You can ask Cortana questions such as current weather and traffic conditions, local points of interest such as closest or popular places to eat, you can find sports scores and biographies.

You can find Cortana by clicking in the search bar.

If you haven't already, you will be prompted to sign in with your Microsoft account details.

Enter your account details and click next.

If this is the first time using Cortana, she will ask you for your name. Type your name into the text box provided then click enter.

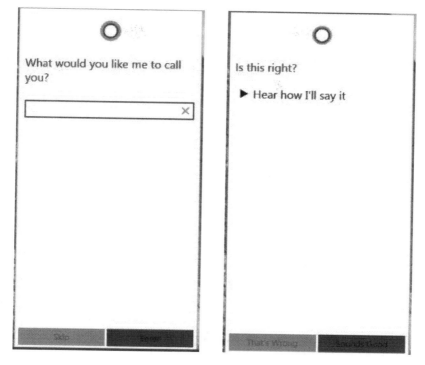

Cortana will ask you if she's pronounced your name correctly, click 'sounds good' if she has. If not click 'that's wrong' and pronounce it for her.

Talk to Cortana

Tap/Click the microphone icon and try some of these voice commands.

You may need to change some of the names.

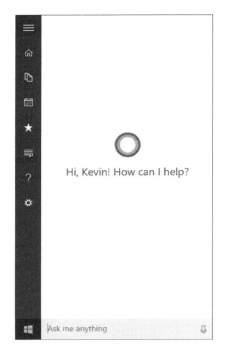

"Call Sister at home"

"Send text to Sophie: When are you coming to play?"

"Create a meeting with Claire at 2pm tomorrow"

"Take Note: Pick up kids, take dog for walk, feed kids, buy milk and ice-cream on way home"

"Show me restaurants nearby"

"What's the forecast for this weekend?"

"Remind me to take the kids out"

"How do I get to Liverpool One?" or *"Show me directions to Liverpool One."*

Other Features

Cortana also has some extra options located on the tool bar down the left hand side of the window.

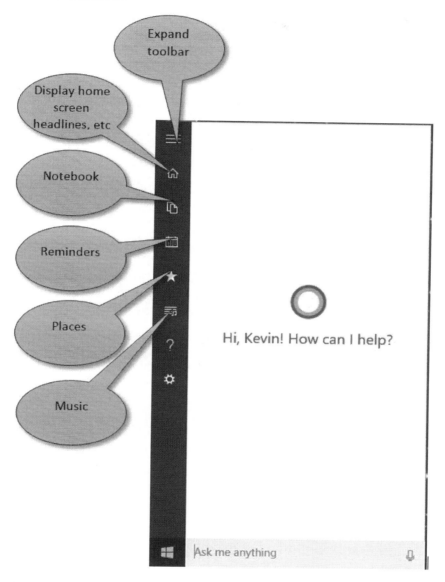

Notebook is Cortana's book of information about you. You can add and edit areas of interest from your daily routine, news and headlines, music, weather, food, lifestyle and more.

Tap the notebook icon on the tool bar and tap the add sign on the bottom right to add an interest. Or tap the ones that are already in the list to edit them.

Tap reminders and Cortana will show you any pending tasks you have asked Cortana to remind you of.

You can add them using the add button, but you can just ask Cortana to remind you of something simply by tapping the mic icon on the taskbar and say it using your voice.

With places you can add your favourite cities, points of interest and places you visit often. This can also help you get directions. Tap the places icon on the tool bar down the left hand side of Cortana's window then tap the add button on the bottom right and type in a place name.

With Cortana music, she can identify music playing just by listening. She will then search for it. Can be a useful feature if you hear a song and what to know what it is or where you can get a copy.

Just tap the music icon on the tool bar and she begins listening...

Customise Cortana

You can customise Cortana in the settings pane.

To do this, click the settings icon on the tool bar circled below.

From here you can change your name and set different preferences.

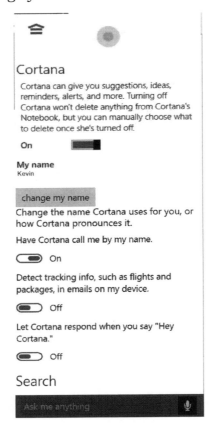

To activate the voice command to get Cortana's attention. Go down to "Let Cortana respond when you say 'Hey Cortana!'"

If you set this to On, you can start talking to Cortana by calling her by her name rather than clicking on the microphone icon.

Microsoft Edge Web Browser

Codenamed "Spartan", Microsoft Edge is built for the modern web and is a more lightweight web browser and replaces Internet Explorer in Windows 10.

It no longer supports ActiveX controls which makes it a little more secure and integrates with Cortana assistant and OneDrive, it also has annotation tools and reading modes.

Lets take a look at what Edge looks like

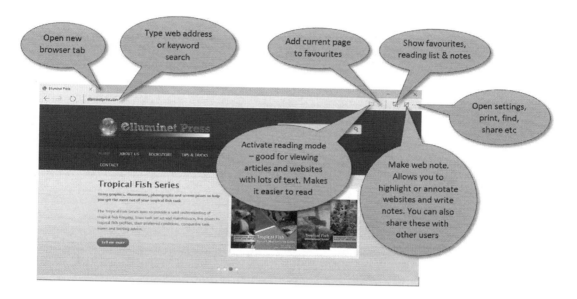

Bookmarks

You can quickly bookmark the page you are on by clicking on the star icon on the tool bar.

In the dialog box that appears type in a name for the website and select 'choose and item' under 'create in'. Select 'favorites'.

You can also create folders to organise your favourites. Click on 'create new folder' and enter a name in the 'folder name' field.

Now when you bookmark any site, click 'choose an item' under the 'create in' field and you will be able to select the folder you created. This will allow you to organise your bookmarks into groups.

To revisit your bookmarked sites click your favourites list icon (circled above).

Annotations & Notes

You can enter annotation mode by clicking on the icon on the tool bar

You will notice a new tool bar appears along the top of your screen.

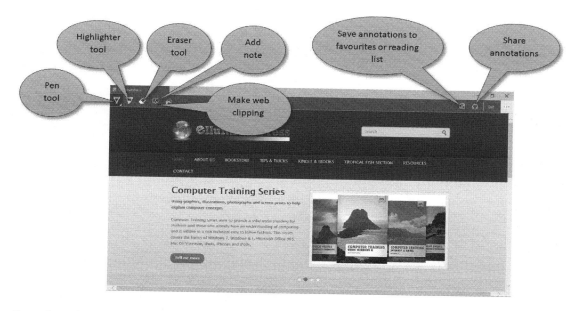

Starting from the left hand side of the tool bar, you have a pen tool.

The next icon across is a highlighter pen.

An eraser tool that allows you to rub out annotations you have drawn.

A note tool that allows you to type annotations in if you can't had write them.

A web clipping tool that allows you to copy a section of the webpage including your annotations to the clipboard where you can paste into a word processing or note taking application.

Pen Tool

Select the pen tool and draw with your mouse or finger/stylus (if using touch interface), then select a colour and pen thickness (size).

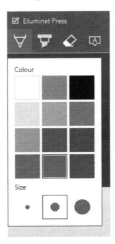

Draw directly on the web page as illustrated below.

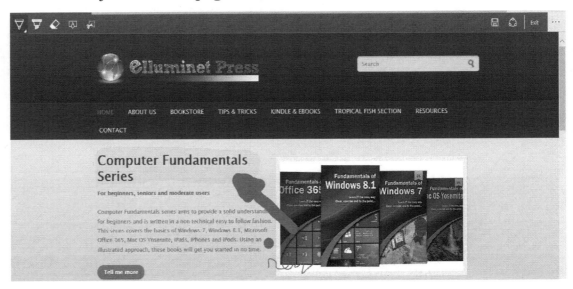

Highlighter Pen

Use the highlighter tool to highlight different words, paragraphs etc on the web page.

You can also select colours and thickness of your highlighter from the drop down menu.

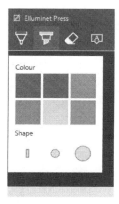

You can draw directly on the screen with your finger or stylus to highlight any text as shown below

There is also an eraser tool so you can rub out any annotations you have made.

Notes

You can also add typed notes with the next icon across. Click the note icon then click on the web page where you want the note to point to.

Then type your notes in the text box that appears.

You can save or share all these annotations using the two icons on the right hand side of the tool bar.

Use the first icon to save the annotations into your favourites or reading list. You can also use the second icon to share your annotated web page via email, print it out etc.

Reading Mode

Some websites, especially those with a lot of text can be difficult to print or read on screen.

Edge has a reading mode that can be quite useful when reading articles on websites.

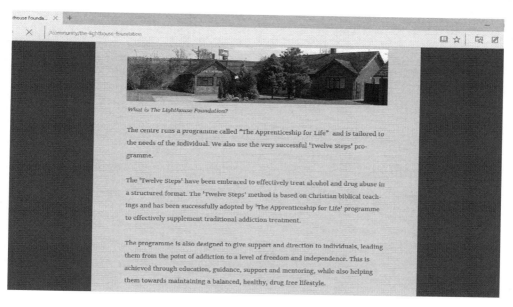

Also some websites do not print particularly well since they are designed to be viewed on screen. So by using the reading mode you can print your website article in a more printer friendly fashion.

More Options

There are some hidden menu options in Edge that you can access by clicking on the 3 dots on the far right hand side of the screen. This will reveal a drop down menu

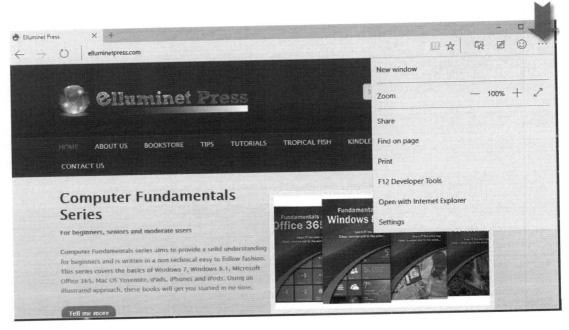

From the menu, you can print the current page, make the text bigger using the zoom function.

You can share the current web page via email or social media by clicking 'share'.

You can search for a particular word on the current web page by clicking 'find on page'.

You can print the current page.

You can adjust settings such as security and privacy etc

Print a Page

You can print the current web page by clicking 'print' from the 'more options' icon indicated below

If you click print from the menu, you will see another dialog box appear asking you what printer you want to print to and number of copies etc.

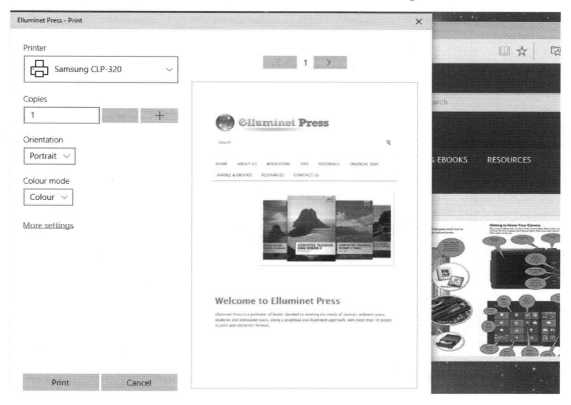

Select the printer from the printer box, enter number of copies if needed.

You can also print portrait or landscape

Select colour mode or black and white

Click print when you are happy with the preview of the printed page shown on the right hand side.

Notifications Centre

The notification centre shows alerts and messages from different applications. These notifications could be email message that have just arrived, system messages or status alerts from applications.

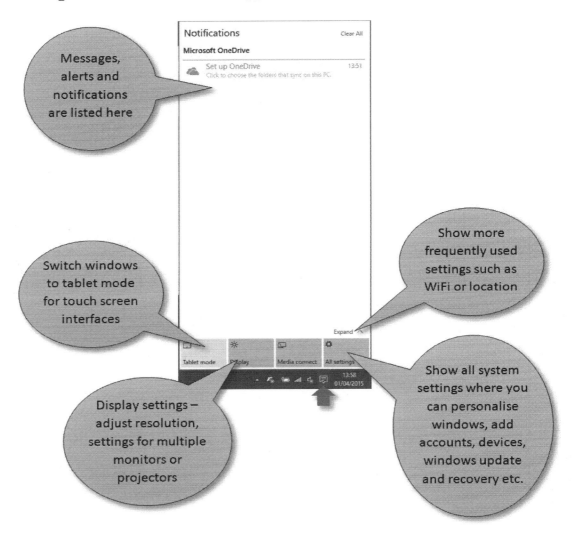

Along the bottom of the notifications window you will see some common settings, eg tablet mode, display settings, media connect for connecting to projectors, second screens etc.

Task View Button

The task view button will show all your currently running apps and display them in thumbnails along the centre of the screen.

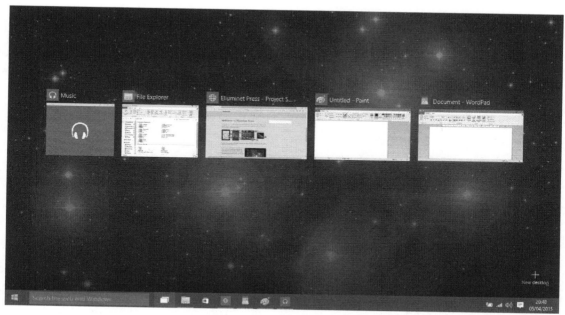

This will allow you to click any of the thumbnails to switch to that app.

Using Multiple Desktops

Multiple desktops is almost like having two or more desks in your office where you can do your work.

You could have a desktop for your web browsing and email, another desktop for your word processing, another desktop for your photo editing and sharing and so on.

Multiple desktops help to organise your tasks together. So you can keep things you are working on together.

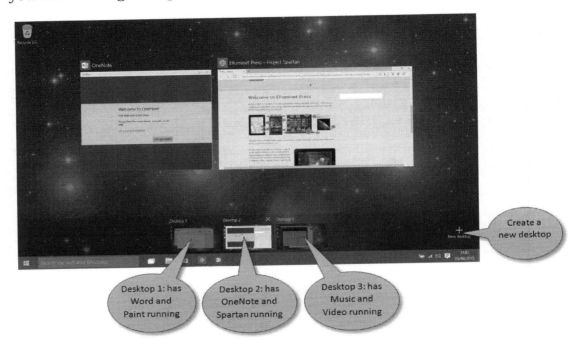

Click on 'new desktop' to open a new desktop then you can open the apps you want to run.

To get a preview of what is running in a particular desktop, hover your mouse over the thumbnails listed across the bottom of the screen. You will see the large thumbnails along the centre of the screen change. This shows you what is running. To switch to an app click on its thumbnail.

To switch between the desktops click on the thumbnails listed across the bottom of the screen (desktop 1, desktop 2, desktop 3 and so on).

Multiple desktops also work particularly well if you have more than one screen connected to your computer. Different desktops can appear on different screens.

Multiple Screens

You can plug in more than one screen into most modern computers or tablets if you have the correct adapters.

You can access your second screen by clicking on the 'notification center' then selecting 'media connect'

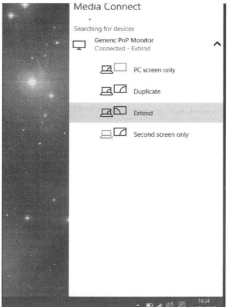

Duplicate PC screen onto Second Screen

Everything you do on the laptop screen will be duplicated on the second screen.

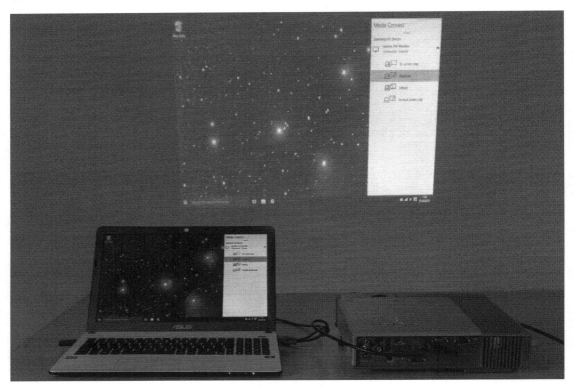

PC Screen Only

This disables the projector and allows the information to be seen only on the PC's monitor.

Extend PC screen onto Second Screen

The second screen acts as an extension to your laptop screen rather than just a duplicate.

This allows you to move windows from the laptop's screen to the second screen and vice versa.

Second Screen Only

This disables your PC's monitor and allows the display to only appear on the second screen.

Photos App

The photos app is a nice little way to organise your photos and works whether you are on a tablet, phone or desktop PC.

It will import photos directly from your digital camera or on-board camera if you are using a tablet or phone.

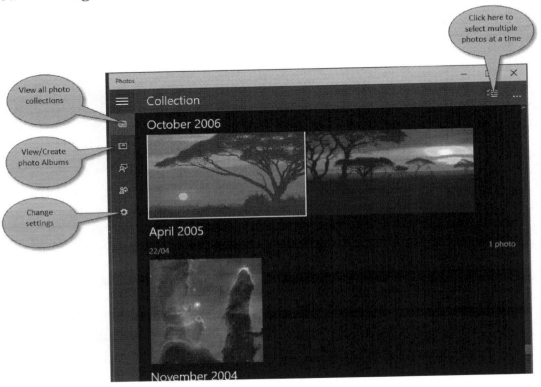

You can also perform minor corrections and enhancements such as removing red-eye, lightening up a dark photograph and apply some simple effects such as sepia or black and white.

To do this, tap or click on an image, this will open the image in view mode.

As you move your mouse or tap on the image a tool bar will appear along the top.

This will give you some options to share a photograph via email or social media, see the image full screen. You can tap the magic want icon to perform some automatic adjustments such as brightness, contrast etc.

You can also tap the pencil icon to do your own editing and photo enhancements.

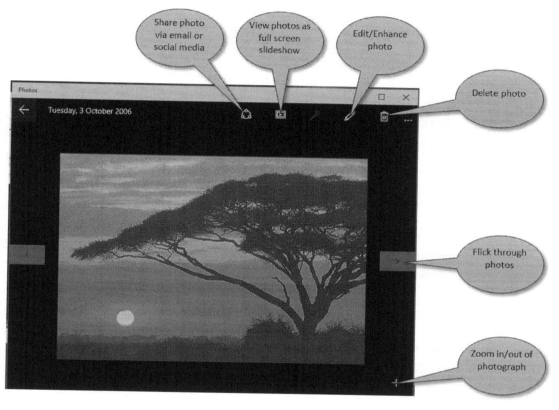

If you tap or click the pencil icon you will enter edit mode.

In edit mode you will see a number of icons appear down the left and right hand sides of the screen.

The functions are grouped by the icons on the left. So for example if you tap basic fixes on the left hand side, all your basic fix tools will appear down the right hand side.

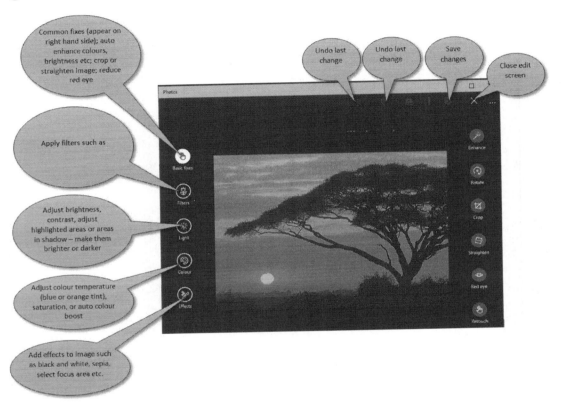

Similarly if you tap or click the 'light' icon, you will see all your options for adjusting contrast, brightness, shadows and highlights appear down the right hand side.

To apply any of these adjustments tap or click on the icons down the right hand side. To adjust drag the large white circle as shown below.

Camera App

The camera app makes use of the on board camera on your phone or tablet to take photographs

Once you have taken your photo you can view them by tapping/clicking the icon on the top left to view in photo app.

In settings you can enable the rule of thirds grid or the golden ratio grid to help you align your photographs.

You can also change resolution and aspect ratio.

Maps App

The maps app is useful for exploring parts of the world, landmarks and famous places. It is also useful for finding driving directions to different locations.

You can search for pretty much any address, country, place or landmark by typing it into the search field.

The maps app has satellite maps, 3D maps and road maps.

Get Directions

You can get driving directions to any location or address you can think of. You can get directions from your current location or you can enter a start location and a destination.

As well as driving directions you can get local bus routes and in some places even walking directions.

To get your driving directions, click or tap the turn-by-turn driving directions icon on the left hand side of your screen, highlighted below.

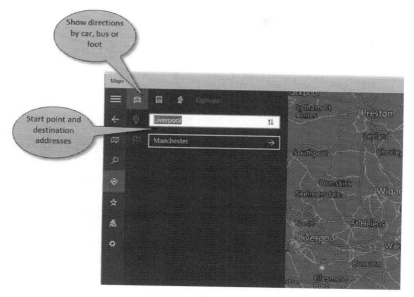

The first field will show your current location (Liverpool in this example). You can also type in a location if you need to.

The second field is where you can enter your destination. This can be a post code/zip code, residential address, town/city or place name.

Once you hit enter or tap the right arrow (next to your destination field), the maps app will calculate a route and display it on a map.

Here you can see your map on the right hand side with a list of driving directions listed down the left hand side.

You can click on any of these directions and the map will zoom in and show you the road on the map.

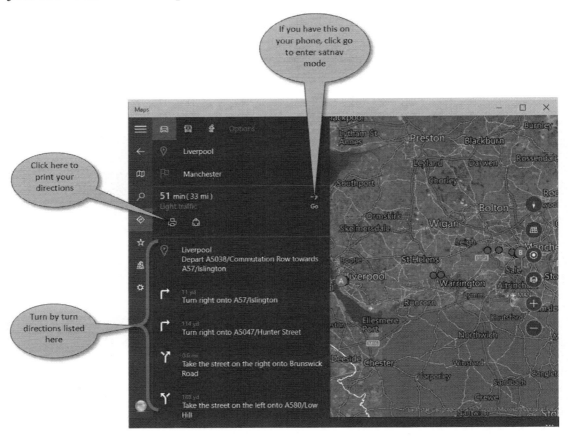

There is also an option to print the directions if needed but if you are using the maps app on your phone or tablet you can use it as a GPS or SatNav and the maps app will direct you as you drive.

Explore in 3D

This feature can come in hand if you want to explore landmarks or areas of interest.

Down the left hand side you will see a number of famous landmarks and areas you can explore in 3D. Perhaps you are going on holiday/vacation and you wan to explore certain parts of the world you haven't been to - just remember the images you see aren't live and can be out of date.

You can have a look by clicking or tapping on the 'explore map in 3D' icon listed down the left hand side of the screen.

Here you can see a fly-over view of a landmark. You can zoom in and out, rotate the map and move around as you explore.

Try also searching for your favourite place by typing it into the search field.

Mail App

You can start the Mail App by tapping or clicking on the mail icon on your start menu.

If this is the first time you are using this app, you may be asked to add your email account.

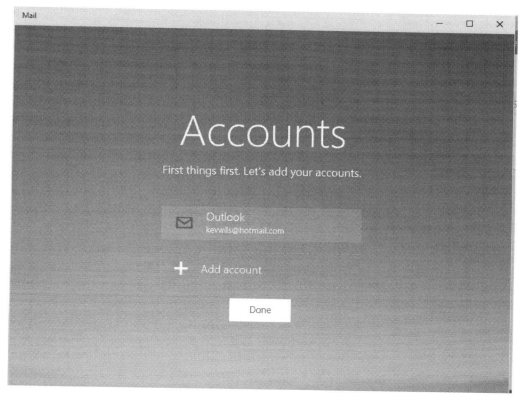

If you are using your Microsoft Account, mail app usually finds it as shown above.

Select this email account and click done.

Adding Other Email Accounts

If you have another email account such as googlemail or yahoo you can add these too.

To do this click the settings icon on the bottom left of the screen.

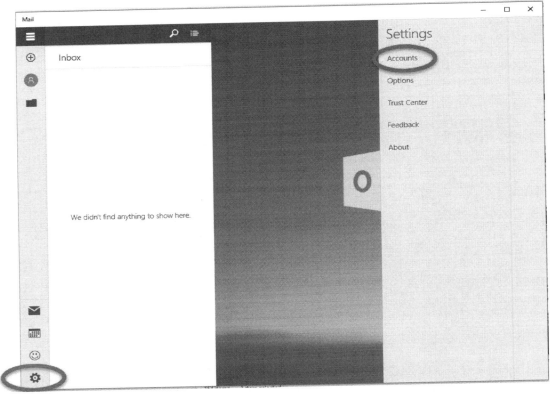

Click 'accounts', then 'add account' and enter the email username and password given to you by the account provider (google, yahoo, apple, etc).

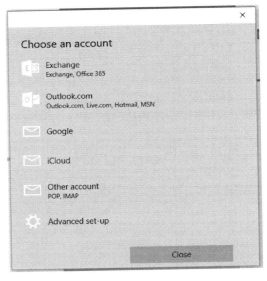

If your provider isn't in the list above click 'other account'.

Using Mail

Once you have done that mail app will check for email, any new messages will appear in your inbox.

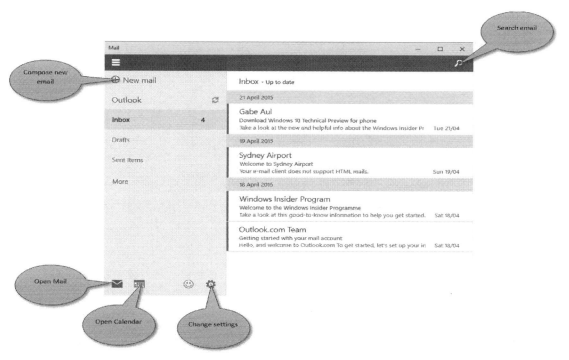

You can open any mail message by double clicking on the message in the list.

Doing this will open a new window where you can reply to the message, forward it or print it.

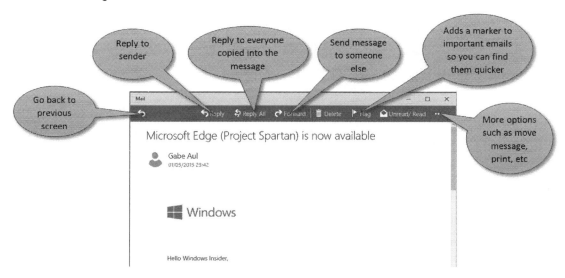

Calendar App

The calendar app links in with the mail app, you can find it on your start menu. It will either have a calendar icon or it will be displaying the current date.

If this is the first time you are using this app, you may be asked to add your email account.

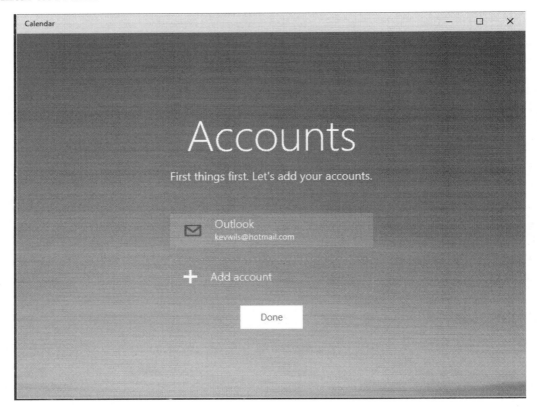

If you are using a microsoft account, calendar app usually finds it for you. If this is the case select the account and click done.

If you use another email account click add account and enter your username/ email and password details given to you by the account provider.

Once you have done that, you will see your main screen.

You can add events and appointments by clicking on the 'new event' button or double clicking on the date in the calendar.

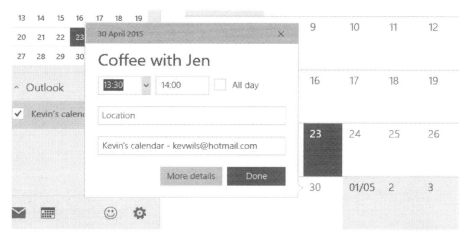

Un-tick 'all day' and enter start and estimated finishing times. Unless it's and all day event.

Type the location where you are meeting.

Music App

When you first start the music app, it will automatically scan your computer for music and add it to your library.

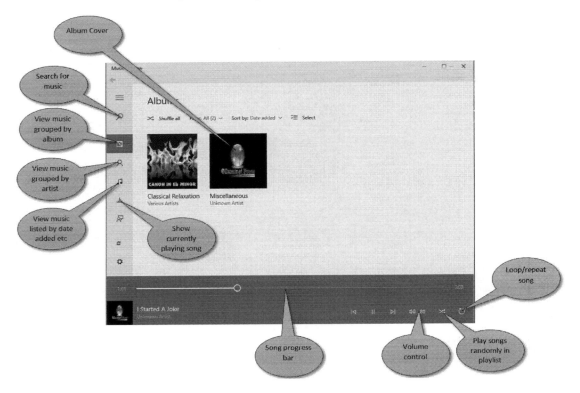

Video App

With the video app you can add and watch your own videos taking with your phone or camera and those downloaded from the internet.

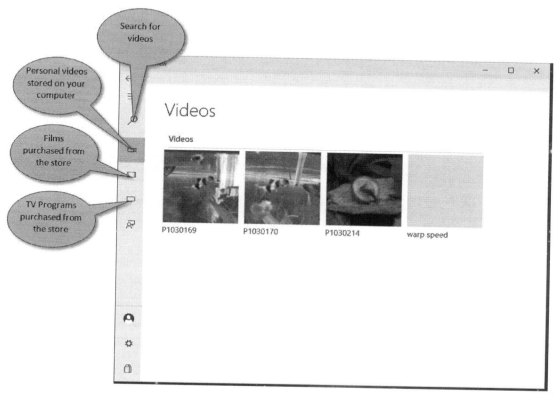

You can also purchase films and television programs and watch them using this app.

Playing DVDs

If you like watching DVDs on your PC, Windows 10 can't them out of the box, so you'll have to download a free player instead.

The best one I found is VLC media player, which can play DVDs, CDs and a range of other file types.

Just go to their website and download the software.

www.videolan.org

Click 'Download VLC', click 'Run' when prompted and follow the instructions on screen

Weather App

The weather app can give you a forecast for your current location or any location you choose to view.

When you first start weather app it will ask for your location, unless you have location services enabled, then it will automatically find your location.

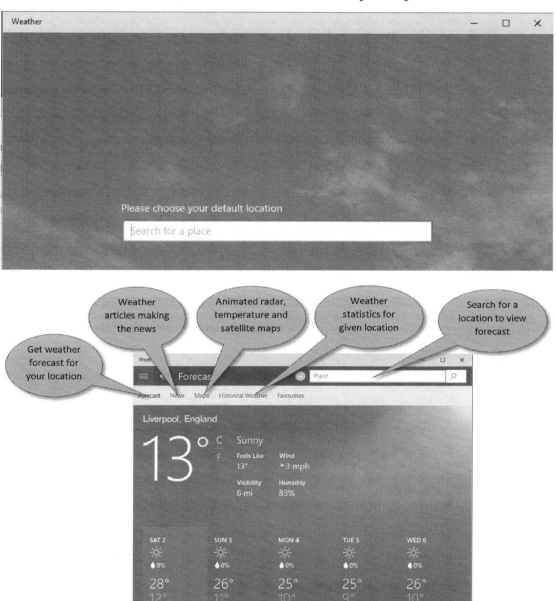

News App

The news app brings you local news headlines and stories from around the world.

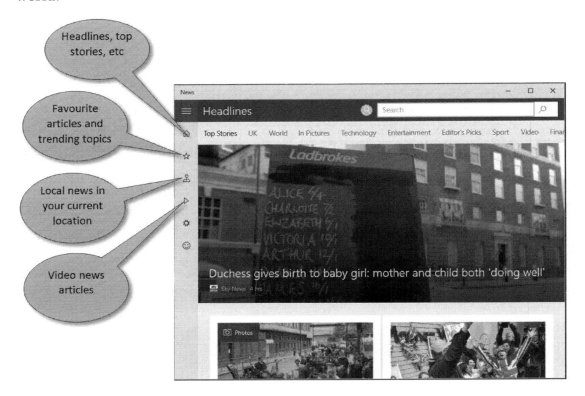

You can read the headlines, or local news, you can also watch video articles and reports.

You can find trending topics and news stories

Health & Fitness App

The health & fitness app is a vast library of workouts and diets as well as a resource of symptoms of illnesses and their possible causes although it would be wise to always consult a medical professional before taking any action.

You can also explore the human body in 3D and find out how all the systems work as well as track your daily diet and exercise routines.

You can completely customise the app to your own personal requirements that will help to analyse your diet, exercise and offer advice and statistics on your progress.

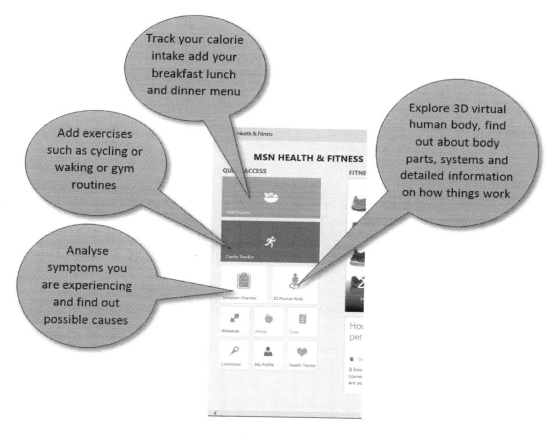

Diet Tracker

With the diet tracker you can add all your foods that you eat for breakfast, lunch or dinner and diet tracker will work out the nutritional value, calorie count etc. Just click '+ Food' and select from the list to add a food to a meal.

Calorie Tracker

The calorie tracker is useful for tracking the calories you burn off during exercises and workouts. You can add different exercises such as biking, running or sports etc add the distance or time and it will keep track of your progress. Just click '+ Cardio Exercise' and select from the list.

Symptom Tracker

The symptom tracker can be useful for finding out different ailments by entering different symptoms and it will give you some possible causes. Still consult your doctor though. Click the '+' sign next to the symptom in the list on the left hand side, then do the same for the list in the centre. Down the right hand side this list will give you some possible conditions of what it could be.

3D Human Body

The 3D human body is a 3D graphic of the body and you can use it to study different systems, such as the digestive system or respiratory system.

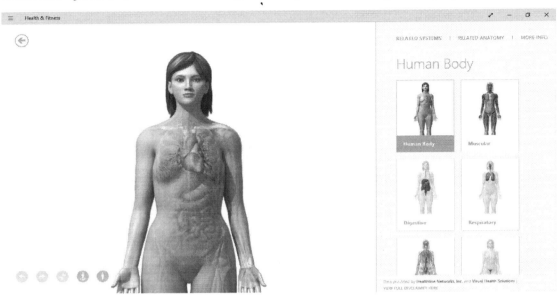

You can use you mouse or finger to zoom in and out or select different parts on the 3D model.

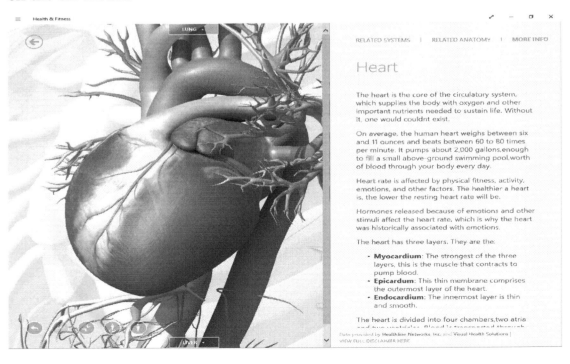

Workouts

The workouts section gives you advice and demonstrates different types of exercises, from simple cardio to weight training.

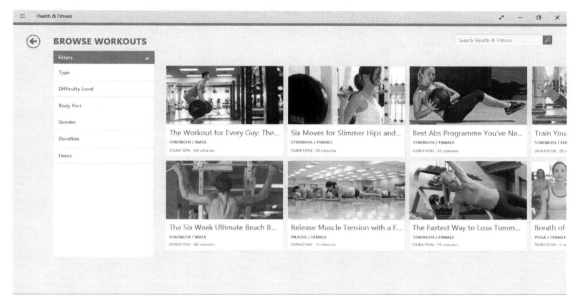

Click on one of the exercises to view details on how to perform the exercise.

Foods

The foods section allows you to look up certain foods such as a chocolate bar or a meal such as lasagne and it will give you a breakdown of the nutritional value, calorie count for different sized servings

Diets

The diets section gives you details on some of the common types of diets such as atkins. You can select different diets from the lists and it will give you information on what foods to eat, what quantities and what to do.

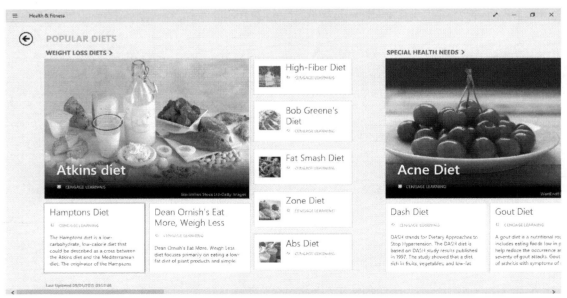

Conditions

The conditions section goes into detail about common ailments such as colds, allergies and diseases. It gives you advice on what causes them, how to treat them and how to protect yourself from them.

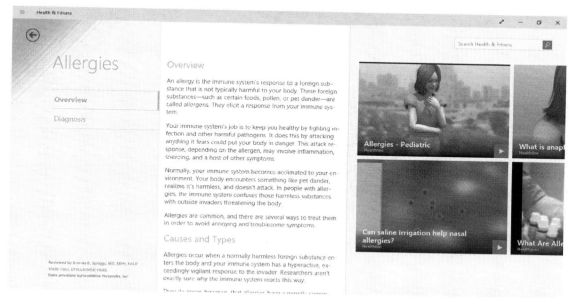

Always good advice to check with your doctor.

Profile

The profile section allows you to enter your personal details such as age, gender, height, weight etc. This allows the health app to correctly monitor your progress and work out calorie counts, appropriate exercise and diet suggestions.

Health Tracker

This section allows you to track your progress. It allows you to enter your weight on a regular basis and tracks your progress over time.

App Store

You can purchase and download a wide variety of Apps for productivity, games, as well as film and television programs directly from the App Store.

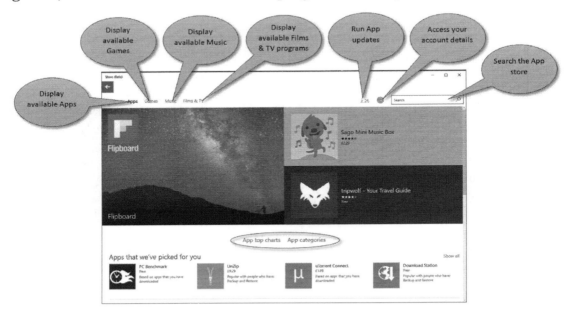

Some Apps and games you will need to pay for so you'll need to add payment details and others Apps and games are free.

If you click 'Apps' you will see a list of popular or trending apps.

Click 'App categories', circled above, and you will see a list of apps broken down in to categories such as kids and family for children's apps and things for them to do, productivity for apps such as office.

You can also search for specific types of apps by using the search field on the top right of the screen.

To buy an app, click on the App's icon to show a summary of what the app is and what it does.

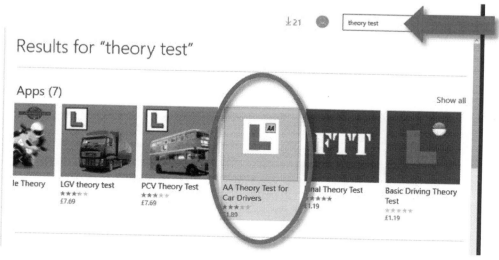

Click the price tag, circled above to purchase and download the app. You may need to enter your Microsoft Account email address and password.

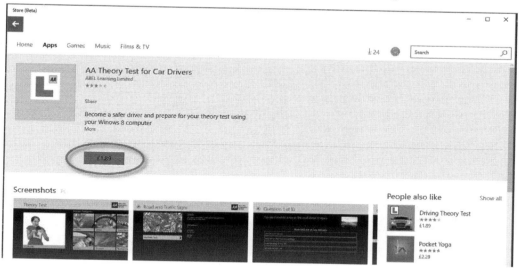

Once the app has downloaded and installed, you will be able to start your app using the start menu.

'Windows Hello' Authentication

Windows Hello is Microsoft's biometric authentication platform that works by scanning your face, iris, or fingerprints to verify your identity, replacing the password to sign into your account.

Passport is Windows Hello for the web. You can log into online services like email, social media and enterprise software instantly and relax with the added security of your device instantly locking if someone else tries to use it.

At the moment most machines won't be able to use Windows Hello face recognition, since you will need specialised hardware such as Intel's RealSense camera that is capable of infra-red photography. Windows Hello will still support existing fingerprint readers.

Chapter 4

Computer Maintenance

Computer maintenance keeps your computers in a good working order.

Using antivirus software, backing up files, keeping your computer up to date.

Also more technical issues such as file defragmentation, disk cleanups and startup programs.

System backup and recovery procedures and advice when your has problems.

Here we will take a look at some common areas and procedures to keep your machine running smoothly

Anti-Virus Software

A lot of this software is sold pre-installed on the machine you buy and is offered on a subscription basis. So you have to pay to update the software.

There are some however that are available for free to home users.

Windows Defender

Windows 10 comes pre-installed with Windows Defender which is automatically updated by Microsoft subscription free.

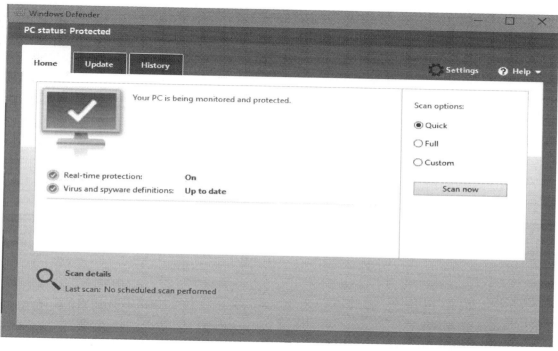

Avast

Avast scans and detects vulnerabilities in your home network, checks for program updates, scans files as you open them, emails as they come in and fixes PC performance issues.

You can download it from their website.

www.avast.com

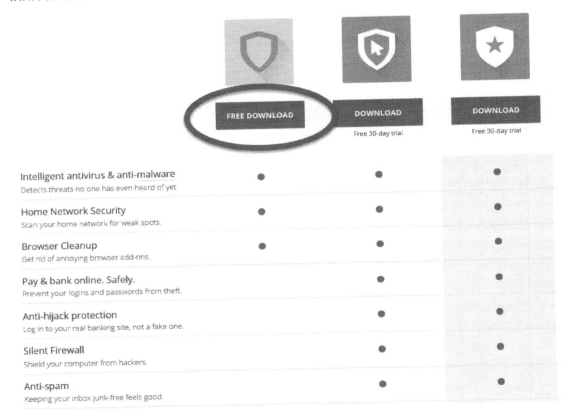

AVG

AVG blocks viruses, spyware, & other malware, scans web, twitter, & facebook links and warns you of malicious attachments.

You can download it from their website.

www.avg.com

Or choose what's best for you	AntiVirus FREE 2015	AntiVirus 2015	Internet Security 2015
Antivirus Blocks viruses, spyware, & other malware	✔	✔	✔
Link Protection Scans web, Twitter®, & Facebook® links	✔	✔	✔
Email Protection Warns you of malicious attachments	·	✔	✔
Online Shield Protects you from harmful downloads	·	✔	✔
Data Safe Encrypts & password-protects private files	·	✔	✔
More Frequent Auto-Updates Get automatic security updates every 2 hours	·	✔	✔
Anti-Spam Keep your inbox free of spam & scams	·	·	✔
Shopping Protection Shop & bank safer with Enhanced Firewall	·	·	✔
Money-Back Guarantee Buy without risk! If you're not satisfied in the first 30 days, we'll refund your money. Learn more	FREE Download	FREE Trial Buy Now	FREE Trial Buy Now

Backing Up your Files

If you have ever lost data because of a computer glitch or crash you know how frustrating it can be. So we all need a good backup strategy. I'm going to go through the strategy I have found that has worked well over the years.

First of all go buy yourself a good external hard disk. This is a small device that plugs into a USB port on your computer. Below is a typical specification for an external hard disk

Plug in your external drive into a free USB port.

In the search field on the task bar type 'file history'

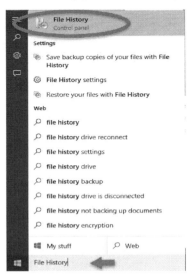

Click 'File History' circled above

On the screen that appears, click 'Turn On' to enable File History

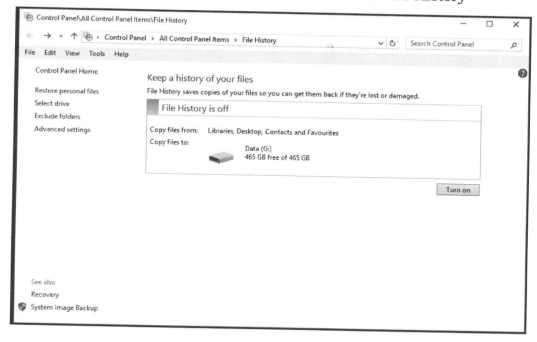

Once you have turned on File History, Windows 10 will start to copy files from your libraries (documents, pictures, music etc) onto your external hard drive.

By default File History saves files every hour but you can change this by clicking on "Advanced Settings" listed down the left hand side of the screen.

A good guide is to set how often File History saves files to "Daily". This will tell File History to save copies of your files once a day.

Good practice would be to plug in your external drive at the end of each day to back up what you have done throughout the day.

Backups can take a while depending on how much you have done.

Restoring Files

Plug in your external Hard drive. Open up File History and click 'Restore Personal Files'

Use the left and right arrows at the bottom to navigate to the date backed up when you know your file still existed or was working.

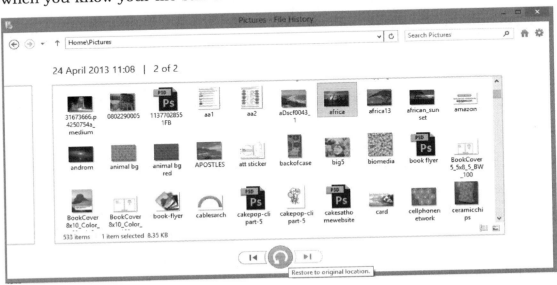

Then in the library section double click in the folder the file was in eg pictures if you lost a photo.

Select the photo and to restore it click the green button at the bottom of the window.

Windows Update

Windows update usually automatically downloads and installs all updates available for windows

This automatic installation can sometimes be a nuisance if you are working and windows wants to download and install updates all the time. You can set it to manual install so you can decide when to install updates. If you don't want to worry about I would leave it on auto.

If you want to change the settings, click settings on the start menu.

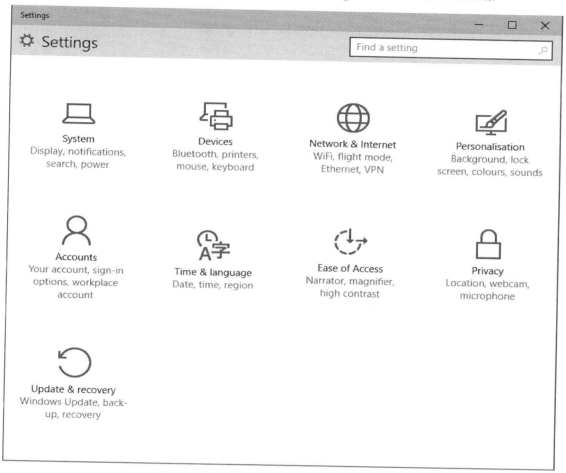

Select 'update & recovery', then select 'Advanced Options'

To prevent windows automatically installing updates select 'download updates but let me choose whether to install them'

Windows will now download all available updates but it will ask you when it's convenient to install them.

Disk De-fragmentation

Data is saved in blocks on the surface of the disk called clusters. When a computer saves your file, it writes the data to the next empty cluster on the disk, even if the clusters are not adjacent.

This allows faster performance, and usually, the disk is spinning fast enough that this has little effect on the time it takes to open the file.

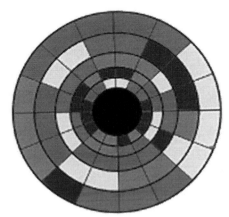 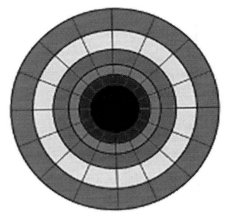

Fragmented Files   **De-Fragmented Files**

However, as more and more files are created, saved, deleted or changed, the data becomes fragmented across the surface of a disk, and it takes longer to access.

This can cause problems when launching software (because it will often load many different files as it launches) so bad fragmentation just makes every operation on the computer take longer but eventually fragmentation can cause applications to crash, hang, or even corrupt the data.

To de-fragment the disk in Windows 10 activate the search and type 'defragment'. Click 'Defragment and optimise your drives'.

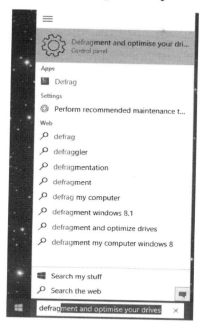

Select the drive your system is installed on, this is usually C. Click optimize

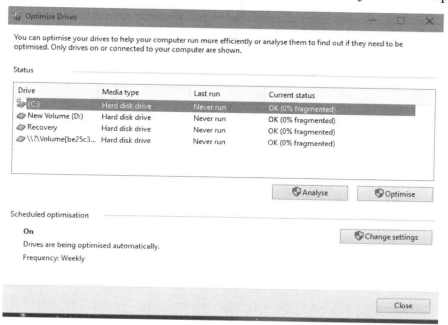

This will start de-fragmenting your disk.

Disk Clean-Up

Over time, windows gets clogged up with temporary files from browsing the internet, installing and un-installing software and general every day usage.

Using the search on the taskbar, type 'cleanup'.

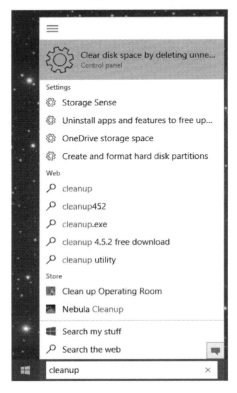

Click 'clear disk space by deleting unnecessary files'

Select drive C, click ok.

In the window that appears you can see a list of all the different files and caches. It is safe to select all these for clearing.

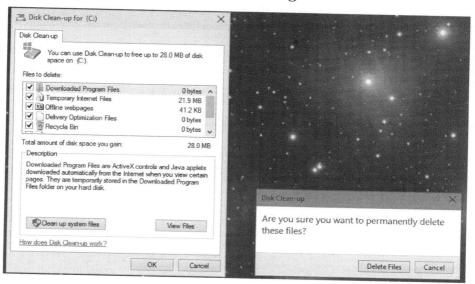

Once you are done click ok and windows will clear out all those old files.

Start-Up Programs

Hit control-alt-delete on your keyboard and select task manager from the menu. Click more details if you don't have the screen below.

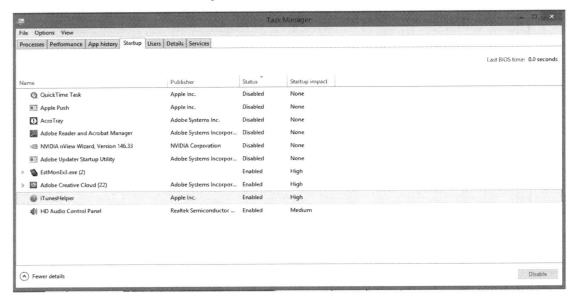

Click on the startup tab. Most of these programs can be disabled with the exception of your sound, video and network devices.

You will also see the startup impact this shows how much the program slows the machine down. These are the programs that show up in your system tray on the bottom right hand side of your screen. As you can see below this system is quite clean – only essential icons appear in the tray.

If you are using a touch device you can access Task Manager by tapping the Search option on the start screen and type Task Manager. Then tap Task Manager in the list that appears.

System Recovery

If you are having problems then Windows 10 has a section to recover your computer

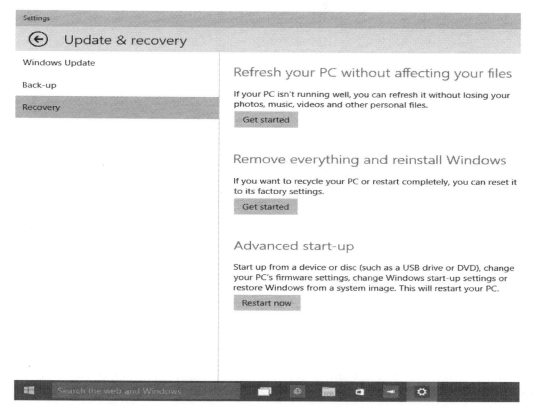

Refresh your PC Without Affecting your Files

This is a useful feature if your PC starts crashing, running slowly and generally non-responsive.

The refresh feature is designed to re-install window's core system without erasing any or your files.

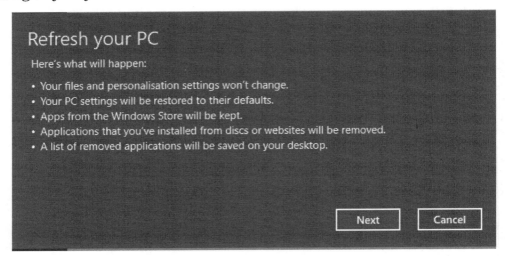

Click next. Windows will show you a list of applications that you will need to re-install. So before you continue with this option make sure you have the necessary disks or downloads for these applications.

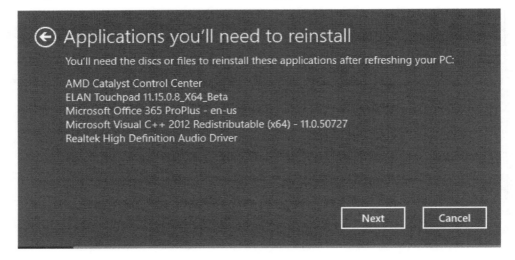

Remove Everything & Re-install Windows

This option will erase everything stored or installed on your system, so use with care.

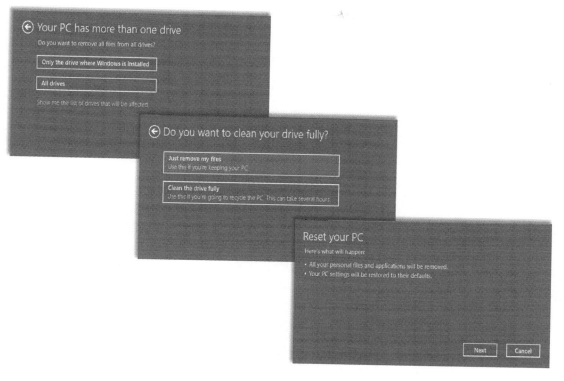

Once you click 'next' windows will restart and the re-installation will begin.

Advanced Start up

This option gets a bit more technical but if you click 'troubleshoot', go to 'advanced options'; a couple of useful features are 'system restore' which restores your PC to a previous state, for example if you installed a driver and its causing problems in windows.

Also 'System image recovery' if you created a recovery image disk. This can be used to restore windows from the image recovery disk.

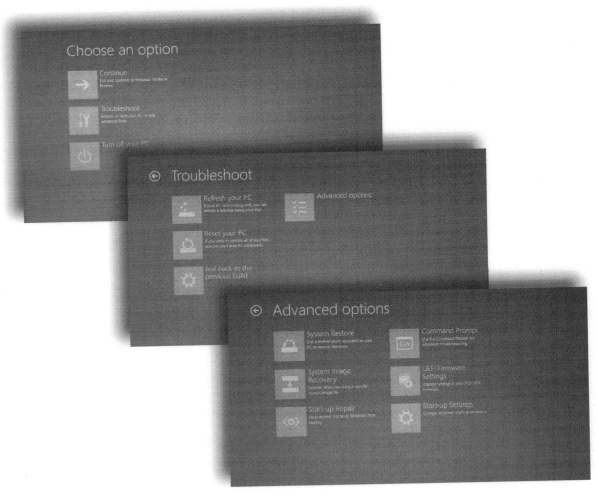

Insert your recovery disk and click 'system image recovery' to restore from a disk

Create a Recovery Drive

A recovery drive or recovery disk is an exact copy of your entire system often referred to as a 'system image'. This image contains your operating system (windows 10), settings/preferences as well as any applications.

This is useful if your computer crashes and you can't start it up again.

From Cortana's Search type 'backup and restore'

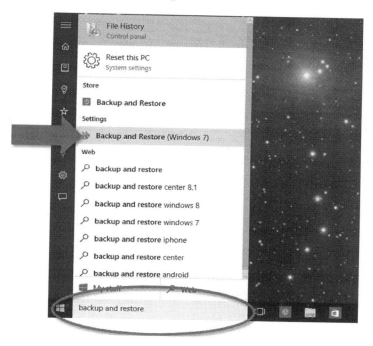

Plug in a portable hard drive (a 500GB capacity is usually enough)

Click 'Create a system image', then select "on a hard disk".

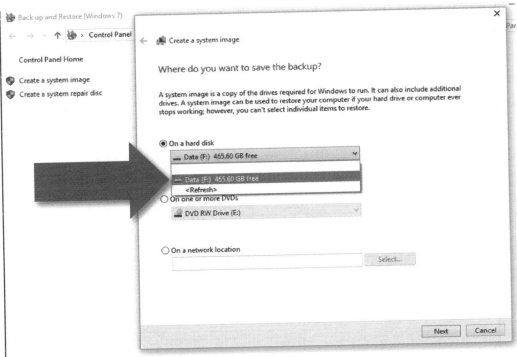

Click next. Make sure only 'system reserved', 'system' & 'windows recovery environment' is selected. Click next.

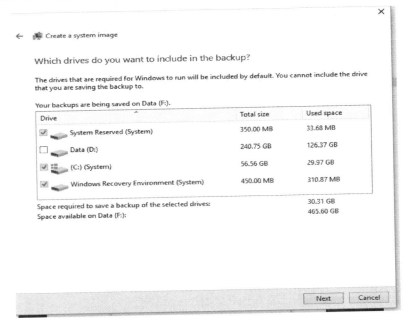

You will be able to start windows with this drive if your computer fails.

Cleaning your Computer

Cleaning Keyboards

To clean your keyboard, unplug it from the computer, use a soft cloth dabbed with rubbing alcohol (or diluted washing up liquid) and run the cloth over the keys to remove all the dirt.

To clear dirt from in between the keys, a can of compressed air is a good way to do this.

Cleaning Computer Mice

First unplug your mouse from the computer.

Most mice are known as optical mice meaning they use a beam of light or a laser to track the movement. To clean these is simple. Unplug your mouse then with your paper towel use your alcohol to wipe the optical window, shown by the arrow below

Also notice the bits of dirt circled above. Make sure you clean this with your cloth using rubbing alcohol or washing up liquid.

Cleaning your Monitor

Modern LCD screens can be quite fragile on the surface so take care when cleaning the screen.

First unplug your monitor from the mains power and with a soft cloth dampened with some diluted washing up liquid start to gently wipe the surface making sure you remove dust and finger marks etc.

Dealing with Spills

If you spill liquid on a keyboard, the best thing I found to do is quickly shut down the computer, disconnect the keyboard from your computer and hold it upside down over a sink and allow the liquid to drain.

If the liquid is a fizzy drink, tea or coffee, you will need to hold the keyboard on its side under warm running water to rinse off the sticky liquid.

At this point, the keyboard may not be repairable, but rinsing the sticky liquid off is the only chance for it to be usable again.

You will need to let the keyboard dry thoroughly for a few days before plugging it back in. After this kind of accident some keys may stick. This is difficult to repair depending on how bad the spill was. Fortunately keyboards are cheap now days.

The best way to avoid this situation is to keep drinks away from the computer area.

Made in the USA
San Bernardino, CA
12 August 2015